iMath
Readers

Mummies in the Library:
Divide the Pages

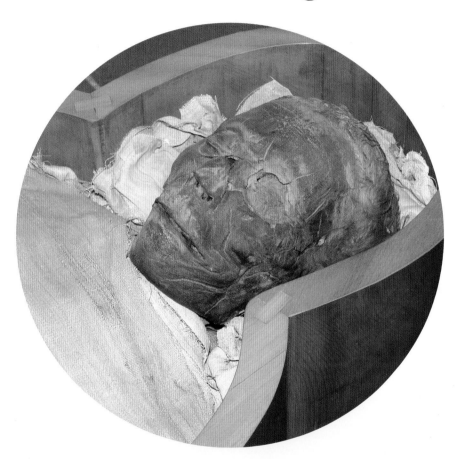

by John Perritano

Content Consultant
David T. Hughes
Mathematics Curriculum Specialist

NORWOOD HOUSE PRESS
Chicago, IL

Norwood House Press
PO Box 316598
Chicago, IL 60631

For information regarding Norwood House Press, please visit our website at
www.norwoodhousepress.com or call 866-565-2900.

Special thanks to: Heidi Doyle
Production Management: Six Red Marbles
Editors: Linda Bullock and Kendra Muntz
Printed in Heshan City, Guangdong, China. 208N—012013

Library of Congress Cataloging-in-Publication Data

Perritano, John.

Mummies in the library: divide the pages / by John Perritano; David Hughes,
content consultant.
p. cm.—(iMath)

Audience: 8–10.
Audience: K to grade 3.
Includes bibliographical references and index.
Summary: "The mathematical concept of division is introduced as a brother
and sister embark on a reading challenge, determining how many pages to
reach each night through different division methods. Different division
methods include using an array, a number line, tally marks, and a division
expression. Includes a discover activity, history connection to ancient
Egypt, and mathematical vocabulary introduction"— Provided by publisher.

ISBN: 978-1-59953-558-6 (library edition: alk. paper)
ISBN: 978-1-60357-527-0 (ebook)

1. Division—Juvenile literature. 2. Reading—Juvenile literature. I. Title.

QA115.P466 2013
513.2'14—dc23
2012023839

CONTENTS

Note to Caregivers:

Throughout this book, many questions are posed to the reader. Some are open-ended and ask what the reader thinks. Discuss these questions with your child and guide him or her in thinking through the possible answers and outcomes. There are also questions posed which have a specific answer. Encourage your child to read through the text to determine the correct answer. Most importantly, encourage answers grounded in reality while also allowing imaginations to soar. Information to help support you as you share the book with your child is provided in the back in the **Additional Notes** section.

Bold words are defined in the glossary in the back of the book.

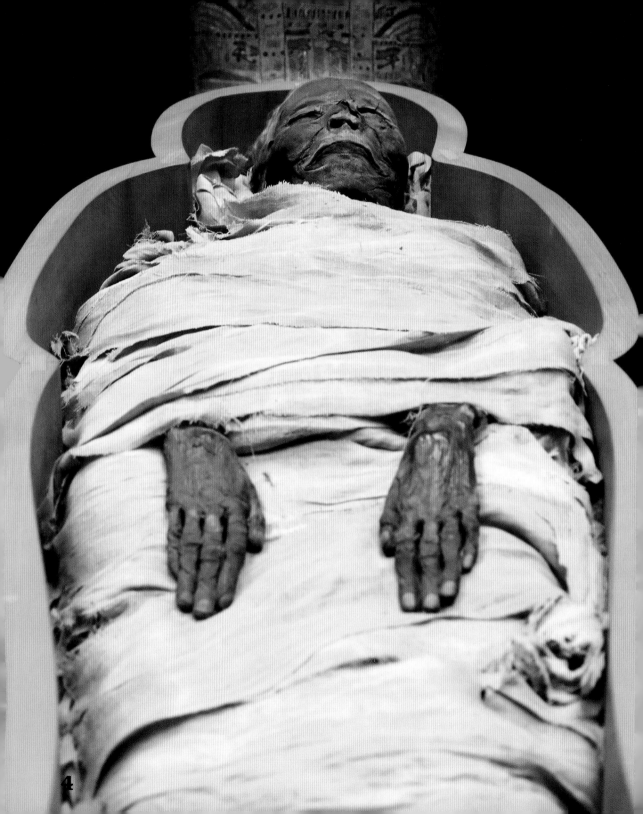

Mummy's the Word

Guess what the mummy did in the library?

It got wrapped up in a book!

Snicker, snicker.

In my family, there are lots of mummies who get wrapped up in books. They're not the real mummies wrapped in cloth, of course. Those kinds of mummies can't read. But we have always called mother "mummy." That means I have a mummy, two grandmummies, and four great-grandmummies, and . . . Well, you get the picture.

My mummy, sister, and I are in the library now. I have suggested a "Reading **Challenge**" to my sister. She and I will each choose a book. The book must have at least 150 pages. We must finish the book in 8 days. How's that for a challenge?

Our mummy has promised to help us **divide** to figure out how many pages to read each night. To divide is to put a set of objects into equal groups. Will either of us finish our book?

Divide and Conquer

We have a large town library with lots of books. I like books about ancient Egypt. Egypt is in northeast Africa. That's where my great-grandmummy came from.

I search in the mystery section for books about mummies or **pharaohs**. I find *The Eyes of Pharoah*. Seshta, Horus, and Reya are the book's main characters. Reya is in the Egyptian army. He warns his friends that nomads are going to make war against Egypt. Nomads are wandering people.

Soon after, Reya disappears. Seshta and Horus set out to find him. They face danger as they try to find their friend.

Great! This is exactly the book I want. It has 160 pages! Now I need to figure out how many pages to read each day.

Idea 1: An **array** is a set of objects put in equal rows. I can use an array with 160 blocks to represent the pages in the book. Then, I can make equal groups of 8. That's one group for each day of our challenge.

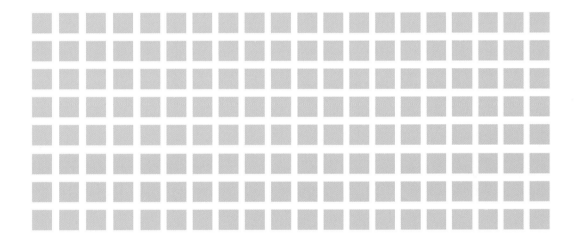

Is this a good way to find out how many pages I have to read each day? Why or why not?

Idea 2: I can use **repeated subtraction** and a **number line** to find the answer. I can start at 160 on a number line. I'll keep subtracting by 8 until I get to 0. I can count how many times I subtract 8.

Do you think this is a good way to find how many pages I must read each day? Why or why not?

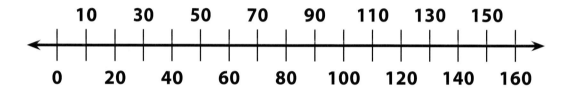

Idea 3: I can draw **tally marks**. I draw one tally mark for each thing I count.

They help me keep track of what I'm counting. If I have lots of tally marks, I put them into groups of five.

Do you think this is a good way to find how many pages I must read each day? Why or why not?

Idea 4: I can write a **division sentence**. For example, I can complete this sentence:

160 pages ÷ 8 days = ___ pages per day.

I can use what I know about multiplication and division to complete the sentence. Do you think this is a good way to find how many pages I must read each day? Why or why not?

160 pages ÷ 8 days = ___ pages per day.

$$160 \div 8 = \underline{}$$

$$8\overline{)160}^{\,?}$$

DISCOVER ACTIVITY

Materials
- a collection of 20 or more objects
- a number cube

Make Equal Groups

Look around the classroom or around your house. Can you find a container with 20 or more broken crayons? Is there a jar of different colored marbles? What about a jar of colorful jellybeans? Go on. See what you can find.

Spill the items you find on a table and count them. How many items do you have in all?

Now, roll the number cube. Divide the total number of objects on the table by the number you rolled. The answer is the **quotient**.

Let's say you roll a 6. Group the objects on the table into groups of 6. How many equal groups can you make? Are any items left over? The items left over are called the **remainder**.

Put all of your objects in one pile again. Roll the number cube. Now decide the best way to find out how many equal groups you can make. Will you:

- build an array?
- use a number line for repeated subtraction?
- draw and circle groups of tally marks?
- write a division sentence?

Solve the problem. Then, choose a different method from the list to check your answer. Do you get the same answer? If you do, the answer is correct! If the answer is different, look back at your work for both problems. Try to find where you might have made a mistake.

Let the Contest Begin

I have my book, but my sister is still looking for hers.
I could get a head start and begin reading. But I don't.
Instead, I look for more books about mummies.

I find a super book! It's called *Mysteries of the Mummy
Kids*. It is about 70 pages long. I want to read
10 pages every day. How many days will it take
to read the book?

Help me use an array to find the answer.

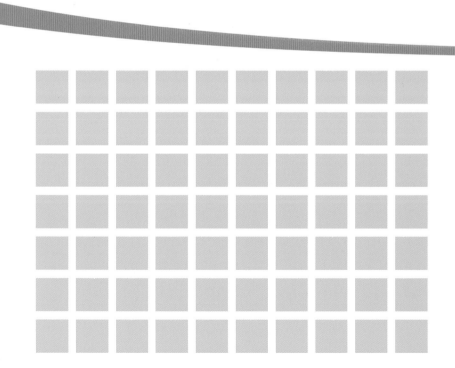

I find another really interesting book. This one is called *Who's Your Mummy?* The book has 160 pages. For this book, I want to read 16 pages a day. How many days will it take me to finish the book?

Use a number line and repeated subtraction to find the answer.

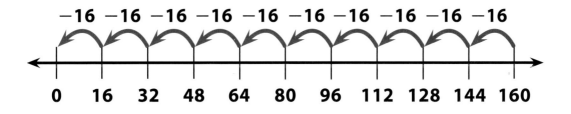

I draw tally marks to check my answer. It takes some time to draw 160 tally marks, but I'm still waiting on my sister. It takes forever for her to choose a book. I probably have time to draw tally marks for every page in every book in the library before she is ready to go.

There Are No Mummies in Baseball

At last! My sister has chosen a book. I'm really disappointed. It's not about mummies. It's not about pyramids. It's not about Egypt at all. It's about baseball.

I should have known. My sister likes baseball. She's a really good pitcher. Once, she struck out three batters in a row. I was one of those batters. Now you know why I don't like playing baseball with my sister. Unless we're on the same team, that is.

If my sister isn't playing baseball, she's reading about it. She chose a book called *The Everything Kids' Baseball Book*. She's looking for different ways to steal a base. I have never found even one way to steal a base.

My sister counts the number of pages in her book. There are about 200 pages in all. I know that's more pages than I have. But really! You should see how many pictures are in her book!

If my sister is going to finish reading her book in 8 days, how many pages will she have to read each day? Help me use multiplication to solve a division problem.

What's the Word?

Mummy's the word if you like being scared. Just read R.L. Stine's *Goosebumps: Return of the Mummy.* You'll learn all about an Egyptian chant that is supposed to bring mummies back to life.

For example, I know that $10 \times 8 = 80$. So, 20 groups of 8 must be 160. How many groups of 8 are in 200?

$$8\overline{)200}$$

$$200 \div 8 = \underline{\quad}$$

I could read twice as many pages as that each day if the book were about mummies.

Mummy's Secret Recipe

Now that my sister has her books, we just have to wait for Mummy. So, I keep reading.

I read that in ancient Egypt, **embalmers** (ehm-BAWLM-urz) used recipes to make mummies. Embalmers treated dead bodies with oils and **natron**. Natron is a salt that dries out and preserves the dead.

When an important person died, embalmers washed the body with oil. They rinsed the oil with water from the Nile River.

I want to travel on the Nile River one day. It is the longest river in the world! It is 4,132 miles (6,650 kilometers) long. Long ago, hippos swam by the river. Crocodiles lived along the river's banks. Hippos don't swim in Egypt's waters anymore. But crocodiles do.

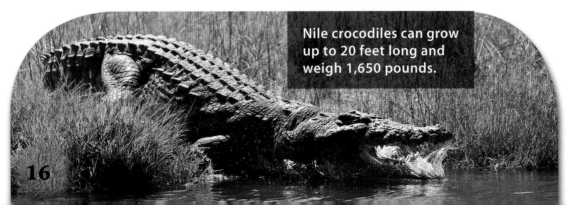

Nile crocodiles can grow up to 20 feet long and weigh 1,650 pounds.

An average crocodile is about 15 feet (4.6 meters) long. I'm almost four feet (1.2 meters) tall. How many of me would it take to be longer than a crocodile? How will you find out?

Next, embalmers removed organs from the body. They used a special hook to pull the brain through the nose. They washed the organs and packed them in natron to dry out.

The embalmer left the heart in the body. At the time, people thought the heart was the center of thinking and feeling. A dead person needed his heart in the afterlife.

After the organs were removed, embalmers stuffed natron into the body and all around the body to dry it out. The salted body was left for 40 days.

How many weeks are in 40 days? Are any days left over? How will you find out?

What's the Word?

In ancient Egypt, the hippo swam in the Nile River and roamed its banks. The Egyptians saw how strong and deadly the animal could be. The hippo became important in their art and religion. The word *hippopotamus* comes from the Greek language and means "river horse."

Jars for the Afterlife

At first, organs taken from a dead body were stored in special jars. Each jar had a head carved into its lid.

The carved heads represented four gods. The falcon held the intestines. The human held the liver. The baboon held the lungs. And the jackal held the stomach.

I find a photo of ancient jars used to hold organs. The jars are in a museum today, but I think about what used to be inside. So cool!

My book says that the museum has 48 jars in all. One fourth of the jars have the head of a jackal. How many jars once held human stomachs? How will you find out?

It's A Wrap

Later on, embalmers didn't store the organs anymore. They dried them in natron. Then, they wrapped them in linen. The jars didn't go away, though. People buried stone or wooden jars with the dead.

After 40 days, embalmers washed the dried body. They smoothed the body with scented oils. The oils included **frankincense** and **myrrh**.

The embalmers stuffed the wrapped organs back into the body. Then, they added leaves and sawdust. The leaves and sawdust helped reshape the body.

Next came the wrapping. Embalmers started with the head and neck. Then, they wrapped each toe separately.

Imagine that it took an embalmer 60 minutes to wrap all of the toes. He spent the same amount of time on each toe. How many minutes did it take him to wrap one toe? How will you find out?

Did You Know?

Did you know that in ancient Egypt, people mummified millions of animals? At the time, people offered the mummies as gifts to the gods.

Egyptians mummified animals like this ram.

Next came the arms and legs. Embalmers put charms between the layers of linen. These charms are called **amulets**. People believed that they kept the body safe on its way to the underworld.

The embalmers worked while a priest read from the *Book of the Dead*. The readings were magical spells. They were supposed to help the dead move safely to the afterlife.

I carry an amulet. It's a four-leafed clover. My sister carries a doll smaller than my little finger. My mummy carries a blue gemstone. She bought it in a rock shop.

The rock shop had a box filled with 200 gemstones. One-fifth of the stones were a shade of blue. How many blue stones were there? How will you find out?

The stones in this picture include blue stones called turquoise and lapis lazuli.

Wrap It Up!

Embalmers tied the mummy's arms and legs together. They put a scroll with magic spells between the mummy's hands. Then, they wrapped the entire body with strips.

After each wrapping, the embalmers painted the strips with a sticky liquid. This glued the strips together. After the last layer, the embalmers wrapped the body with a cloth. Artists painted a god on the cloth.

Osiris was the god of the afterlife, the dead, and the underworld.

Then, the embalmers tied one more cloth around the body. They put a painted mask over the mummy's face. They placed the body and the mask in a coffin. This coffin went inside another coffin and then a third coffin.

In ancient Egypt, it took 70 days to finish making a mummy. If drying took one-half of that time, how many days did it take for a body to dry out? How will you find out?

King Tut's death mask was decorated with gems and colored glass.

Connecting to History

There was an exciting mummy discovery in 1922. It was a tomb! The tomb held the mummy of King Tutankhamen, or King Tut. King Tut was a weak and sickly boy king. He became king at age 9 and died at age 19. Many treasures were buried with him. Even his inner coffin was made of solid gold.

Today, King Tut's death mask is famous around the world. It, too, is made of solid gold.

Many things lay hidden beneath King Tut's wrappings. There was a jeweled circle around the head. There were rings and bracelets on his hands and arms. There were golden sandals on his feet. And there were lots of amulets. They had been made and placed according to the *Book of the Dead*.

Math at Work

Archaeologists are scientists who study the past. They look for clues that tell us how people lived long ago. Sometimes the clues are in the layers of soil. Or they may be things like a piece of a wall or sidewalk. Other clues are objects that people have left behind.

Archaeologists dig to find clues. Before they dig, they mark out squares. These squares usually measure 5 feet × 5 feet (1.5 meters × 1.5 meters). Each square gets a number. Scientists use the numbers in their notes. They also write the number on bags that hold the things scientists find in the ground.

The Great Pyramid of Giza is one of the Seven Ancient Wonders of the World.

Connecting to Engineering

The Great Pyramid of Giza was Pharaoh Khufu's mummy-keeper. In ancient times, a village grew around the tomb. That's because it took 80 years for people to finish building the pyramid!

Up to 30,000 workers built the pyramid. **Engineers** at the time figured out how to cut and pull giant stones from the ground. They figured out how to move the stones. And they figured out how to stack them. The Great Pyramid of Giza is made of more than two million stone blocks. Some of those blocks weigh 15 tons.

Drink Up

Finally, my mummy has her books. I think how much fun it would be to ride home on a camel. You know, like the camels around the Great Pyramid of Giza.

Camels can travel up to 100 miles (160.93 kilometers) in the desert without drinking. But when they are thirsty, they really lap it up! A camel can drink 30 gallons (113.56 liters) of water in 13 minutes!

Imagine a **caravan** of 8 *really* thirsty camels. Together, they drink 136 gallons (515 liters) of water. If they each drink the same amount of water, how many gallons of water do they each drink? How will you find out?

How Many Pages?

Once we reach home, I ask my mummy for help. "I have 8 days. How many pages must I read each day if I am going to finish my book?"

We think about the problem. And we think about ways we could solve it.

Idea 1: "You could build an **array**," my mummy says. I know she is right. Building an array would work well. But I would need to find or draw a lot of objects to find the answer. No, I think, building an array will take too long.

Idea 2: So, my mummy asks if I want to use **repeated subtraction**. Yes, I could definitely do that. But I would need a **number line** to help me. And it would take some time to draw it and label it correctly. No, I think, repeated subtraction will take too long.

Idea 3: "What about using **tally marks**?" my mummy asks. Yes, I could certainly do that. But it would take a long time to draw 160 tally marks and then group them. That is a lot of tally marks. No, I think, tally marks will take too long.

Idea 4: "Okay," says mummy. "What about completing a **division sentence**? Let me show you what I mean." Mummy writes the sentence for me.

160 pages ÷ 8 days = ___ pages per day

I finish the sentence.

$$8\overline{)160}$$

How many pages must I read each day? Do you think I will be able to do it? I had better start reading!

WHAT COMES NEXT?

You can make your own mummy. But don't practice on your friends or pets. Use an apple instead. It's an easy and fast way to see how mummies were made.

Here's what you need:

- apple
- plastic cup
- baking soda
- salt
- mixing cup
- bowl

Here's what to do:

- Divide the apple into four pieces.
- Put one apple slice in a plastic cup.
- Mix 1 cup of baking soda with 1 cup of salt.
- Pour the mixture over the apple slice in the cup.
- Store the cup in a dry, dark place.
- Eat the rest of the apple.
- Check back in a week.

What did you notice? The apple dried up. Its skin turned brown. Congratulations. You're a mummy maker.

GLOSSARY

amulets: charms.

archaeologists: scientists who study the past.

array: a set of objects organized in equal rows.

caravan: a train of pack animals, like camels.

challenge: a task or event that tests someone's skills.

divide: to put into equal groups; to find how many things are in each group; to find how many groups there are in all.

division sentence: a number sentence that uses division.

embalmers: people in ancient Egypt who made mummies.

engineers: people who use machines and technology to do their work.

frankincense: sap from a kind of tree that grows in parts of Africa and Arabia.

myrrh: sap from a kind of tree that grows in parts of Africa and Arabia.

natron: a salt used to dry the organs and body of a dead person.

number line: a diagram that uses points on a line to represent numbers.

pharaohs: Egyptian kings.

quotient: the result you get when you divide.

remainder: the amount left over after you have finished making equal groups.

repeated subtraction: to use a number line to subtract by a number a certain number of times.

tally marks: marks made to help you count.

FURTHER READING

FICTION

The Headless Mummy, by David Keane, HarperCollins, 2007

The Missing Mummy, by Ron Roy and John Steven Gurney, Random House Books for Young Readers, 2001

NONFICTION

Mummies, by Dana Meachen Rau, Benchmark Books, 2010

National Geographic Kids Everything Ancient Egypt: Dig Into a Treasure Trove of Facts, Photos, and Fun, by Crispin Boyer, National Geographic Children's Books, 2012

ADDITIONAL NOTES

The page references below provide answers to questions asked throughout the book. Questions whose answers will vary are not addressed.

Page 9: 20 pages

Page 12: $70 \div 10 = 7$ days

Page 13: $160 \div 16 = 10$ days

Page 15: $200 \div 8 = 25$ pages

Page 17: $15 \div 4 = 3$ body lengths with 3 feet left over. $40 \div 7 = 5$ weeks and 5 days

Page 18: $48 \div 4 = 12$ jars

Page 20: $60 \div 10 = 6$ minutes

Page 21: $200 \div 5 = 40$ blue stones

Page 22: $70 \div 2 = 35$ days

Page 26: $136 \div 8 = 17$ gallons

Page 28: $160 \div 8 = 20$ pages

INDEX

CONTENT CONSULTANT

David T. Hughes

David is an experienced mathematics teacher, writer, presenter, and adviser. He serves as a consultant for the Partnership for Assessment of Readiness for College and Careers. David has also worked as the Senior Program Coordinator for the Charles A. Dana Center at The University of Texas at Austin and was an editor and contributor for the *Mathematics Standards in the Classroom* series.